mA

A Kid's Guide to
INCREDIBLE TECHNOLOGY™

The Incredible Story of Trains

Greg Roza

The Rosen Publishing Group's
PowerKids Press™
New York

For Marcus

Published in 2004 by The Rosen Publishing Group, Inc.
29 East 21st Street, New York, NY 10010

First Edition

Editor: Kathy Kuhtz Campbell
Book Design: Mike Donnellan

Illustration Credits: Alessandro Bartolozzi and Roberto Simoni; p. 8 diesel train illustration by Mike Donnellan.
Photo Credits: p. 4 © Hulton-Deutsch Collection/CORBIS; pp. 7 (left), 7 (right) 8, 12 © Bettmann/CORBIS; p. 11 © Georgina Bowater/CORBIS; p. 16 © John F. Mason/CORBIS; p. 19 © Robert Holmes/CORBIS; p. 20 © Astier Frederik/CORBIS SYGMA.

Roza, Greg.
The incredible story of trains / Greg Roza.
    v. cm.— (A Kid's guide to incredible technology)
Contents: The power of steam—Electric power—Diesel power—Combining engines—High-speed trains—Getting up to speed—Bogies and brakes—High-speed tracks—What did that sign say?—Flying trains of the future.
  ISBN 0-8239-6712-3 (library binding)
1. Railroads—Trains—Juvenile literature. [1. Railroads—Trains.] I. Title. II. Series.
  TF148 .R69 2004
  385—dc21   2002154592
Manufactured in the United States of America

Contents

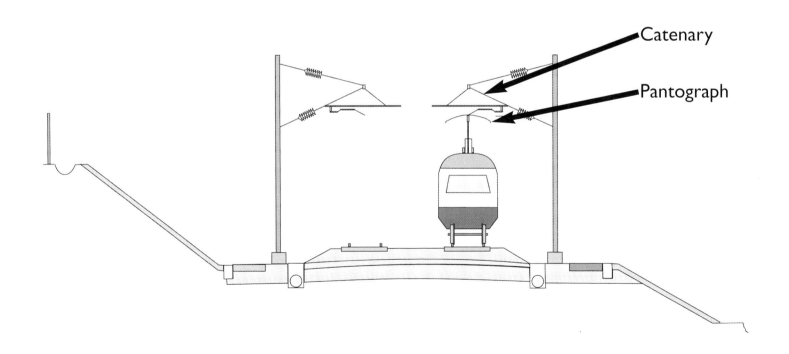

Catenary

Pantograph

Steam and Electricity

Train **technology** can be traced to the mid-1500s, but the first modern **locomotives** were made in the early 1800s. They ran on steam that was produced on the train. In 1879, Werner von Siemens of Germany made the first train powered by electricity. Electricity for an electric train is made in a **power plant**, not on the train. There are two ways by which electricity leaves the power plant. One way is by a third rail that runs along the other two rails on a track. A shoe, a metal tool under a train, conducts electricity from that rail to the train's motors, which turn the wheels. The other way electricity leaves the plant is through a **catenary**, a wire that hangs over the train on poles placed along the tracks. A **pantograph** sits on a train's roof and touches the catenary as the train moves. Electricity travels down the catenary to the pantograph and then to the motors.

Left: *In 1829, George Stephenson of England made a steam engine for his Rocket that was used as a model for all future steam engines.* Right: *The first electric train, built by Werner von Siemens, carried passengers at the Berlin Trade Fair in 1879.* Bottom: *Today electric trains such as this one use catenaries and pantographs.*

5

Diesel Power

Fuel is something that is burned to provide heat or power. Many train engines are powered with a kind of fuel oil called diesel fuel. Rudolf Diesel of Germany wanted to produce a more useful engine than the steam engine. He made the first diesel-powered engine in 1893. Diesel based his engine on a power **cycle** that uses four strokes of the **pistons** to create power. The pistons move down, up, down, and up in one cycle. The pistons draw air into the **cylinders** and compress it. Compress means to press hard. Compressing the air makes it very hot, about 1,000°F (537.8°C). Diesel fuel is sprayed into the compressed air. This action causes an explosion, which forces the pistons down and creates power for the train. As the pistons move back up, they push the burned gases out of the cylinder. The pistons are connected to rods that turn the wheels and make the train move.

Left: Rudolf Diesel was born in France but moved to Germany in 1890 to work in a machine factory. For more than 13 years, he worked on his idea for a more useful engine that would not make thick clouds of soot as did a steam engine. Right: Diesel's first diesel-powered engine, a test engine, was made in 1893.

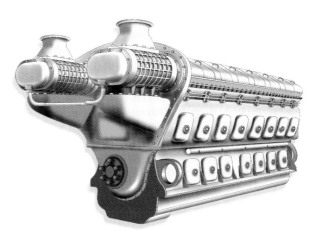

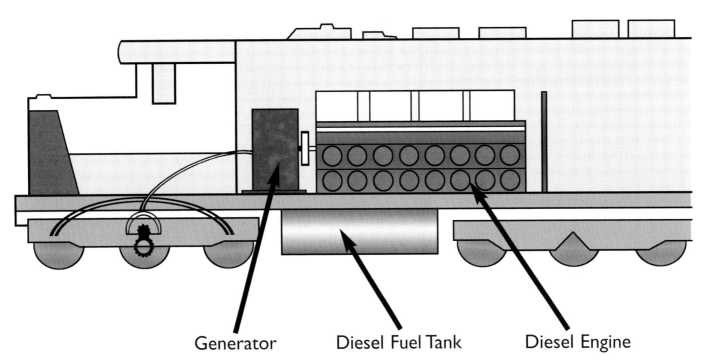

Generator   Diesel Fuel Tank   Diesel Engine

Combining Engines

In the early 1900s, electric train systems were expensive to make. They needed large amounts of electricity, long wires, and **generators** to power the trains. Early diesel engines were not practical because of their large size. The 1920s saw the creation of an improved pump that sprayed the fuel into the cylinder and a new engine that used two strokes instead of four for the power cycle. This smaller engine, a **hybrid** engine usually called a diesel engine, uses both diesel and electric power. This diesel engine powers a generator on board the train, which creates electricity. The electricity runs the motor on each axle, which turns the wheels to make the train move. By 1961, diesel locomotives had completely replaced steam trains. Diesel engines were more expensive to build, but they were sturdier, lasted longer, and caused less harm to the tracks.

Top Left: *In 1934, the first diesel-powered train for travelers, the steel Pioneer Zephyr, sped 1,000 miles (1,609.3 km) between Denver, Colorado, and Chicago, Illinois, at 78 miles per hour (125.5 km/h), in only 13 hours.* Top Right: *This is what a diesel motor for trains looks like today.* Bottom: *This drawing shows a hybrid locomotive.*

High-Speed Trains

In the past 40 years, countries around the world have produced incredible new technologies that allow trains to travel faster than ever before. Improved engines, tracks, train shapes, and new materials, or what things are made of, help to make modern trains quicker and more comfortable.

On October 1, 1964, Japan introduced to the world the first high-speed train, called the Shinkansen, which means "new trunk line" in English. The Shinkansen also became known as the bullet train because of the shape of its nose and because when it travels down a track it looks like a speeding bullet. The first Shinkansen traveled at an average speed of 100 miles per hour (161 km/h) and reached a high speed of 130 miles per hour (209.2 km/h). Today Shinkansen trains connect 15 cities all over Japan. They can travel about 160 miles per hour (257.5 km/h).

Top: *One of France's high-speed trains, called the TGV, zooms by a field of sunflowers.* Bottom: *This kind of Shinkansen bullet train was built from 1995 to 1998. It has a long nose, a dome window to give the driver a great view of the track, and soundproofing inside to lessen the riders' sense that they are moving fast.*

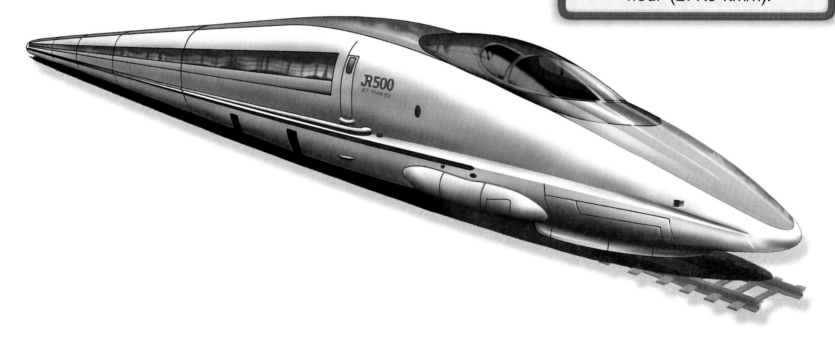

TECH KNOWLEDGE

When two high-speed trains going in opposite directions pass each other on tracks that are side by side, the wind caused by the trains can cause them to slow down or even to run off the rails. For this reason, the tracks of high-speed trains are laid farther apart than those of regular trains so that the trains can pass each other safely.

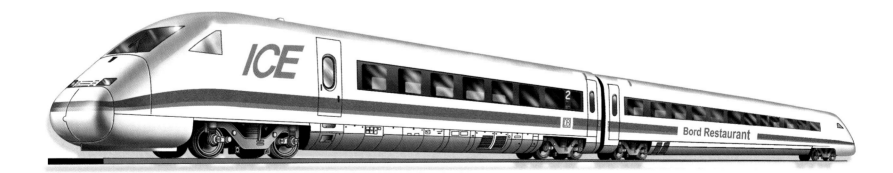

Getting Up to Speed

High-speed trains must be as light as possible. Many trains are made of steel, but some are made of lighter metals to help increase their speed. A high-speed train in Germany called the ICE, or InterCity Express, is made of a light metal called **aluminum**. Older trains, such as the 1955 French locomotive CC7107, have a square or an uneven shape. The ICE has a sloped and rounded nose and an **aerodynamic** shape. The ICE train has 2 engines and 12 cars. The cars of the ICE are close together to reduce the amount of wind that can get caught between them. This design allows air to flow over the surface of the train smoothly, reducing the amount of wind resistance. Wind resistance is the force of air against a moving train that limits its motion. All these aerodynamic parts help the newest ICE trains to run up to 240 miles per hour (386.2 km/h)!

Top: *The French CC7107 train set a world speed record of 206 miles per hour (331.5 km/h) on March 28, 1955. Notice its square front, which is not as aerodynamic as the front of today's high-speed trains.* Bottom: *Though it can go faster, Germany's ICE train today travels up to 186 miles per hour (299.3 km/h) safely.*

Trains That Tilt

High-speed trains such as the Shinkansen were made to travel on straight paths. Turns can cause high-speed trains to slow down. Some high-speed trains, such as those in Italy, Sweden, and the United States, use special cars that tip called tilting cars to help keep their speeds as high as possible. In the United States, Amtrak's Acela has six cars, each of which has its own special tilting system. Without the tilting system, the Acela, which travels up to 165 miles per hour (265.5 km/h), would cause the people who are riding on the train to feel the force of a turn. That would make a very uncomfortable ride. As a car enters a turn in the tracks, the tilting system measures the turn and the speed of the car. An instrument in this system sends these facts to a special computer on the car which then tilts that car to the correct angle so that the ride feels level.

14

Top: *These drawings show the difference in force that a person riding in a train feels when the train has a tilting system. A rider feels more force without the tilting (left) than with it (right).* Bottom: *The Acela has six cars. Each car has a tilting system. The train's driver receives directions about speed and safety through the rails.*

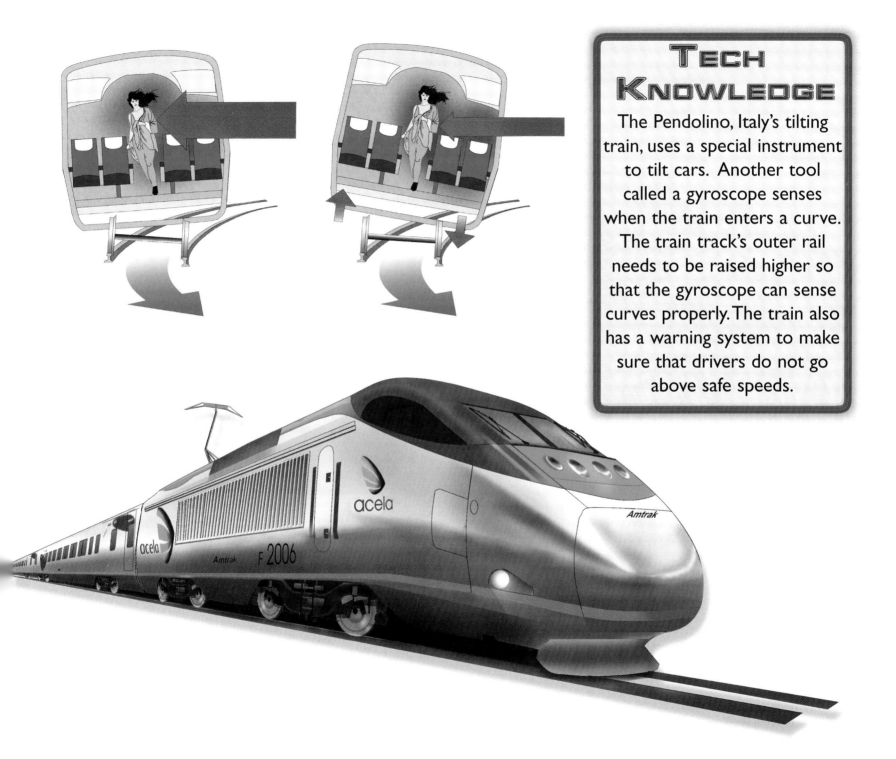

TECH KNOWLEDGE

The Pendolino, Italy's tilting train, uses a special instrument to tilt cars. Another tool called a gyroscope senses when the train enters a curve. The train track's outer rail needs to be raised higher so that the gyroscope can sense curves properly. The train also has a warning system to make sure that drivers do not go above safe speeds.

acela

Amtrak

acela

Amtrak   F 2006

Bogie Frame   Motor   Motor   Disc Brake   Wheel

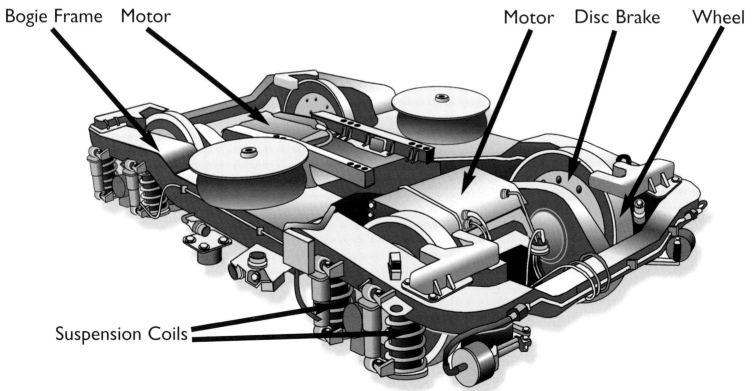

Suspension Coils

Bogies and Brakes

A **bogie** is a strong metal frame that connects the wheels and axles of a train. Bogies keep the wheels, motors, brakes, and **suspension** coils, or springs, in place. Two bogies can support each car, as in the Shinkansen. The bogies can also be shared, as in the French TGV. The back end of one TGV car and the front end of the next TGV car share one bogie. As for brakes, some high-speed trains use disc brakes. Each axle has four metal discs surrounded by special padded tools called clamps on them. When a driver uses the brakes, the clamps close on the discs. This causes the discs, axles, and wheels to slow down. Most trains also have tread brakes, which are special blocks that fit on the outside of the wheel where the wheel touches the track. When in use, tread brakes press against the turning wheels. After disc brakes have slowed a train, tread brakes are used to stop it.

Top: *The cars on the Spanish Euromed share bogies. Besides being coupled together, the cars are joined by the bogies.* Bottom: *This illustration shows a Shinkansen bogie. In addition to the motors, suspension coils, and brakes, each bogie on the Shinkansen contains four wheels. Two bogies drive each car forward.*

High-Speed Tracks

When planning a high-speed railroad system, builders first need to decide the best route to follow. A train can travel faster when there are fewer turns in the track, so builders try to select straight, flat land on which to build the tracks. Once the route has been cleared and leveled, a layer of gravel is put down to support the tracks. Sleepers, or ties, which are usually **concrete** blocks, are laid on top of the gravel. Thin pieces of steel track are attached to the sleepers. The steel tracks are connected from end to end by using heat to melt the steel, creating a pair of long tracks on which trains can travel.

To make a railroad as straight as possible, builders sometimes need to construct bridges to go over rivers and valleys, or tunnels to go through mountains or under rivers. This takes the most time and is the most expensive part of building a rail system.

Top: *The track for a high-speed train, such as this Shinkansen train in Tokyo, Japan, must be laid on flat land.* Bottom: *These two drawings show the track systems for high-speed trains. The right drawing shows two concrete blocks with steel sleepers. The left one shows a track system that uses a concrete sleeper to support the rails.*

Tech Knowledge

A high-speed rail system called Eurail connects the cities of Dover, England, and Calais, France. The Eurostar, the train that travels on this line, moves up to 186 miles per hour (299.3 km/h). The Eurostar is limited to 100 miles per hour (160.9 km/h) through a tunnel that was built beneath the English Channel. The Channel Tunnel is 31 miles (49.9 km) long, making it the world's longest tunnel.

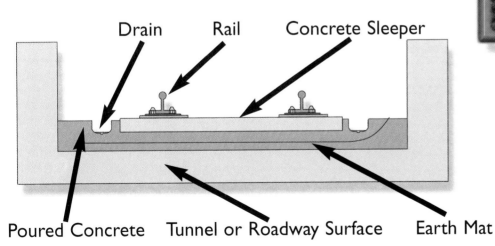

Drain   Rail   Concrete Sleeper

Poured Concrete   Tunnel or Roadway Surface   Earth Mat

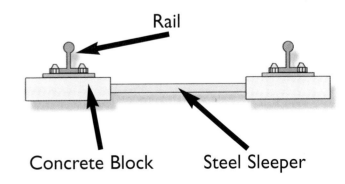

Rail

Concrete Block   Steel Sleeper

TIMELINE

1825 George Stephenson of England builds the first successful steam-powered train for freight and riders.
1879 German inventor Werner von Siemens makes the first train powered by electricity.
1893 Rudolf Diesel makes the first diesel test engine.

1934 The first diesel-and-electric train runs between Denver and Chicago.
1964 Japan introduces the first high-speed train, or bullet train, called the Shinkansen.
1972 The first TGV train, a gas-powered test model, runs at 198 mph (318.7 km/h).

1988 The first ICE train, an electric-powered test model, sets the world speed record at 252 mph (405.6 km/h).
1990 The electric TGV Atlantique sets the world speed record at 320 mph (515 km/h).
2003 In China, a German-made maglev begins service and reaches its top speed of 266 mph (428.1 km/h).

What Did That Sign Say?

Regular railroad systems use signs and lights to warn train drivers when there are other trains on the same track. This is called signaling. The drivers of high-speed trains, however, have trouble seeing this signaling as the train zips by at top speeds. High-speed trains use a new technology called continuous cab signaling. The signaling is passed through the track itself in the form of electricity. A computer in the cab of the train picks up the signaling and displays it on the driver's computer. The computer then gives the driver a report about the section of track on which the train is traveling. This includes the speed limit for that section of the track, speeds of other trains on the same track, and how far away those other trains are. If the train is going too fast, an alarm sounds to warn the driver.

The control panel in a TGV driver's cab is connected to a main control center where people watch all the trains on the system. When two trains are running on the same track, someone at the control center uses a computer to tell the two trains' drivers how fast each should go and how close the two trains are to each other.

Flying Trains of the Future

China, Japan, Germany, and the United States are creating a new type of high-speed technology called maglev. Maglev stands for magnetic **levitation**. Maglev trains use a **magnetic field** to float between ⅜ and nearly 4 inches (1–10 cm) above their tracks. This technology has done away with noisy wheels and the bumps of trains traveling on steel tracks. The world's first maglev train, a German-made maglev, began service in Shanghai, China, in January 2003. It ran a length of 19 miles (30.6 km) and reached its top speed of 266 miles per hour (428.1 km/h).

Scientists in Japan are also working on the Aerotrain. The Aerotrain will have two sets of wings and will travel in a roofless, concrete tunnel rather than on tracks. At 300 miles per hour (482.8 km/h), the Aerotrain will float on a cushion of air from 2 to 4 inches (5–10 cm) thick. By using the Aerotrain technology, which combines train and aircraft improvements, scientists can give riders faster, cleaner, and cheaper ways to travel.

Glossary

aerodynamic (er-oh-dy-NA-mik) Made to move through air easily.

aluminum (uh-LOO-muh-num) A type of metal.

bogie (BOH-gee) A low, strongly built frame that holds two axles and four wheels on a train.

catenary (KA-tuh-ner-ee) A wire strung between poles alongside high-speed train tracks that carries the electric power for the train.

concrete (KON-kreet) A mix of water, stones, sand, and a special gray powder. Concrete becomes very hard and strong when it dries.

cycle (SY-kul) A course of events that happens in the same order over and over.

cylinders (SIH-len-derz) The containers in which pistons move in an engine.

generators (JEH-nuh-ray-terz) Machines that change motion into electrical energy.

hybrid (HY-brid) Something that is a mixture of two different things. A hybrid train is powered by a diesel engine that turns an electric generator.

levitation (leh-vuh-TAY-shun) The act of rising and floating in the air.

locomotives (loh-kuh-MOH-tivz) Powered train cars, which move the rest of the cars over tracks.

magnetic field (mag-NEH-tik FEELD) The area around a magnet where its pull is felt.

pantograph (PAN-tuh-graf) A metal pole, attached to the roof of a high-speed train, that draws power from the catenary for the electric motors.

pistons (PIS-tunz) Sliding parts in an engine that are moved by a gas or a liquid.

power plant (POW-ur PLANT) The machinery needed to produce power.

suspension (suh-SPEN-shun) A system of machines, such as springs, that work on car wheels to make a ride less bumpy.

technology (tek-NAH-luh-jee) The way that a people do something using tools, and the tools that they use.

23

Index

A
Acela, 14
Aerotrain, 22

C
catenary, 5
cylinder(s), 6, 9

D
Diesel, Rudolf, 6
diesel fuel, 6

E
electricity, 5, 9, 21
electric train, 5
engine(s), 6, 9–10

H
high-speed train(s), 10,
    13–14, 17, 21

I
InterCity Express (ICE), 13

L
locomotive(s), 5, 9, 13

M
maglev, 22

P
pantograph, 5
pistons, 6

power cycle, 6, 9

R
rail(s), 5

S
Shinkansen, 10, 14, 17
steam, 5–6, 9

T
TGV, 17
ties, 18
tilting system, 14

W
wind resistance, 13

Web Sites

Due to the changing nature of Internet links, PowerKids Press has developed an online list of Web sites related to the subject of this book. This site is updated regularly. Please use this link to access the list:
www.powerkidslinks.com/kgit/trains/

24